D0989102

BLESSINGS for LIFE

WORDS OF HOPE AND HEALING

Sylvia Gunter and
Elizabeth Gunter

© 2017 by Sylvia Gunter

Published by
The Father's Business
P O Box 380333
Birmingham AL 35238
www.thefathersbusiness.com

All rights reserved. Contents and/or cover may not be reproduced in whole or in part without the express written consent of the author.

All scripture quotations, unless otherwise indicated, are taken from the Holy Bible, New International Version®, NIV®. Copyright ©1973, 1978, 1984, 2011 by Biblica, Inc.™ Used by permission of Zondervan. All rights reserved worldwide. www.zondervan.com The "NIV" and "New International Version" are trademarks registered in the United States Patent and Trademark Office by Biblica, Inc.™

Scripture quotation marked (Amplified) are taken from The Amplified Bible, Copyright © 1954, 1958, 1962, 1964, 1965, 1987 by The Lockman Foundation. Used by permission.

Scripture quotation marked (Message) are taken from The Message. Copyright © 1993, 1994, 1995, 1996, 2000, 2001, 2002. Used by permission of NavPress Publishing Group.

Scripture quotations marked (NKJV) are taken from the New King James Version®. Copyright © 1982 by Thomas Nelson. Used by permission. All rights reserved.

Scripture quotation marked (NLT) are taken from the Holy Bible, New Living Translation, copyright © 1996, 2004, 2007 by Tyndale House Foundation. Used by permission of Tyndale House Publishers, Inc., Carol Stream, Illinois 60188. All rights reserved.

Scripture quotation marked GOD'S WORD®, copyright © 1995 God's Word to the Nations. Used by permission of Baker Publishing Group.

Cover and book Design by Jan Metros.

Editorial and production oversight by Leigh Ann Erwin.

Special thank you to AlphaGraphics, 2159 Rocky Ridge Road, Suite 107, Hoover, AL 35216, US448@alphagraphics.com

ISBN 978-1-931379-38-0

Dedication

Receive with your spirit this prayer of Paul for his spiritual children in Ephesians 1:17-19.

"I keep asking that the God of our Lord Jesus Christ,
the glorious Father, may give you the Spirit of wisdom and revelation,
so that you may know him better.
I pray also that the eyes of your heart may be enlightened
in order that you may know the hope to which he has called you,
the riches of his glorious inheritance in the saints,
and his incomparably great power for us who believe."

Be blessed to live in His Spirit of wisdom and revelation.
Be blessed to know Him and His power for you.

© Sylvia Gunter 2017, The Father's Business P.O. Box 380333 Birmingham, AL 35238

Table of Contents

© Sylvia Gunter 2017, The Father's Business P.O. Box 380333 Birmingham, AL 35238

Introduction

The Atacama Desert in Chile is known as one of the driest places on earth. It holds the world record for the longest dry streak, going years without rain. In March 2015 the desert experienced 14 years' worth of rain in one day. That sounds bigger than it was. It was less than an inch of rain, barely enough to make the ground wet in most places. The rain nourished seeds that had been buried for years. A little while later the desert produced an explosion of color—purple, pink, and white flowers as far as the eye could see. The intensity of blooms was unprecedented.

The seeds had been there all the time. They were waiting for just a little rain to bring forth life and beauty. That is what blessing the human spirit is all about. As you bless your spirit and the spirit of others, you are nourishing what God has already planted deep inside. You are calling forth everything that God has placed within you. Imagine less than an inch of rain falling on the desert floor. Those little rain drops hit hard, cracked ground. Most people wouldn't think it was enough rain to make a difference. But it did. What may seem like a few simple words can bring hope and healing to very dry ground in yourself and others.

The concept of blessing your spirit may be new to you. Scriptures about your spirit are throughout the Bible. This introduction will show you the Biblical foundation for using blessing to begin a lifelong adventure of blessing yourself and others.

What is the human spirit?

Your spirit is the essence of who you are. The word for "spirit" in Hebrew is ruach and in Greek it is pneumo, which means breath. Your human spirit is the breath that God breathed into you when He created you. Think about when God created Adam. He took some of the earth and He breathed life into Adam. Your human spirit is that part of you that existed before you had a human body. It will continue to exist after your human body has died (Job 33:4, 34:15).

Zechariah 12:1 says that the Lord stretches out the heavens, lays the foundations of the earth, and forms the human spirit within a person. Let it sink in deeply, how special you are. God who stretched out the heavens and laid the foundations of the earth also formed your human spirit and put it within you.

Jeremiah 1:5 says, "Before I formed you in your mother's womb, I knew you. Before you were born I set you apart." Before you had a body, before you were formed in your mother's womb, God knew you. At some point in eternity God breathed into you and made your spirit. At His chosen time, He knit you together in your mother's womb (Ps. 139:13). He didn't stop there. Job 10:12 says, "You gave me life and showed me kindness, and in your providence watched over my spirit." So God has been watching over your spirit since the beginning.

You have been created spirit, soul, and body in God's image, a beautiful reflection of the Trinity (Gen. 1:26). You are a masterpiece. You were born with the breath of God inside you. Whether you are a believer or not, you have a human spirit. The difference is that as a believer, you are allowing your spirit to be controlled and directed by the Father, Son, and Holy Spirit. God designed your human spirit to be led by the Holy Spirit, allowing God to flow through us and impact the world around you.

Is there a difference between spirit and soul?

Scripture talks about spirit and soul as individual parts. Some godly men whom I admire would say that the words spirit and soul are used interchangeably in scripture. Hebrews 4:12 says, "The Word of God is living and active. Sharper than any double-edged sword, it penetrates even to dividing soul and spirit." If the spirit and the soul are the same, if they are interchangeable, how can they be divided? 1 Thessalonians 5:23 says, "May God himself, the God of peace, sanctify you through and through. May your whole spirit (pneuma), soul (psyche) and body (soma) be kept blameless at the coming of our Lord Jesus Christ." We are a living essence from God (spirit), that He gave an expression (soul) in a tangible physical

© Sylvia Gunter 2017, The Father's Business P.O. Box 380333 Birmingham, AL 35238

package (body). We are a living spirit who has a soul housed in an earthly body. All three are important and have a role to play.

Your human spirit is the innermost part where the Holy Spirit resides. It is the connection point between God and your soul and body. The roles and relationships of spirit, soul, and body are complex and intertwined. It is not possible to give absolute definitions that "this is only spirit, this in only soul, this is only body." It is not that clear-cut. As you read the Bible about spirit, soul, and body, it actually becomes less clear. Some will say that your emotions, your mind, your will, and your memories are your soul. The Bible says your spirit also has emotions, will, and mind. Your body can hold memories and emotions. So it is not so easy to define. Here is the great news: we don't have to. Hebrews 4:12 says that dividing between what is spirit and what is soul is God's job.

In scripture the spirit has a separate existence. The soul and body depend on the spirit to function. Jesus affirmed this as he raised the dead daughter of Jairus. "He took [the girl] by the hand and said, 'My child, get up!' Her spirit returned, and at once she stood up. Then Jesus told them to give her something to eat. Her parents were astonished" (Luke 8:54-56). Her spirit was separate from her body, and her body needed her spirit to live.

According to 1 Corinthians 2:11, the human spirit is able to receive and perceive things from the Holy Spirit. Verse 14 says the soul does not receive the things of the Spirit of God for they are foolishness to him, nor can he know them because they are spiritually discerned. The soul is more limited in understanding and perspective. It is horizontally-oriented, aware of what it sees, feels, and thinks in the present surroundings and circumstances. The human spirit led by the Holy Spirit has access to God's wisdom and revelation that passes all human understanding.

God designed our spirit to stay connected to God's spirit, then for our spirit to lead our soul and body so they work as a team. The relationship of spirit to soul is somewhat like a dance. It is a beautiful partnership, but someone has to lead and someone has to follow. The spirit has the responsibility to lead under the direction of the Father, Son, and Holy Spirit for the benefit of the soul and body.

Several times in Psalms the spirit is speaking to and leading the soul. The most familiar one is "Why are you cast down, O my soul, and why are you disquieted within me? Hope in God; for I shall again praise him, my help and my God" (Ps. 42:5). The psalmist's human spirit is speaking to his own soul. Twelve times in the Psalms you will see this (Ps. 42, 43, 62, 103, 104, 116, 146). The spirit initiates change and leads in God's transformation, and the soul and body respond and add their own unique God-designed contributions. The harmony of the whole is truly beautiful.

Why do we bless?

The Bible was written in and to a culture that was steeped in blessing—the blessing of shalom, blessing the child with His name, the patriarchal blessing to the sons, the blessing of God for His people, the blessing of Jesus and of the disciples.

Something inside everyone craves a blessing. The Hebrew word for "to bless" is baruch. Baruch means "a good word." When we bless someone, we are speaking "good words" of truth about how God sees them and loves them. Blessings are designed to answer those questions we all struggle with at times: Who am I? What am I here for? Do I have what it takes? Am I truly loved? Blessing a person's spirit invites them to find the answers to those questions in God. The most profound blessing we need and can receive is the Father-heart of God, His special creation of us, His kind intention toward us, and His matchless love for us. Some of Father God's best healing work is establishing our true identity in Him. He reveals to us who we really are and affirms and restores us in the image of Christ's glory revealed in us.

Blessing our spirit invites it to its place of priority and leadership over the soul and body. It is a daily, sometimes hourly, invitation. Proverbs 25:28 says, "Whoever has no rule over his own spirit is like a city broken down, without walls." We have to learn to become intentional to live with our spirit leading. It doesn't happen

© Sylvia Gunter 2017, The Father's Business P.O. Box 380333 Birmingham, AL 35238

automatically, it takes practice. It will not feel natural at first because most of us are not taught we have a spirit and how to live from it. We have been living with our souls in charge for a very long time. Ephesians 4:23 (Amplified) describes it as being "constantly renewed in the spirit of your mind" [having a fresh mental and spiritual attitude]. The spirit has the responsibility to lead under the direction of the Father, Son, and Holy Spirit for the benefit of the soul and body. As we recognize and nourish our spirit, our soul and body become healthier and more whole as it takes its proper place in God's design.

Is it biblical to speak to the human spirit?

In Christ as a part of His royal priesthood we are to speak blessing and be a blessing to those around us. Psalm 129:8 says "the blessing of the LORD be upon you; we bless you in the name of the LORD."

Paul blessed the spirits of others in four of his letters written to the early church.

"The grace of our Lord Jesus Christ be with your spirit, brothers. Amen" (Gal. 6:18)

"The Lord be with your spirit. Grace be with you" (2 Tim 4:22).

"The grace of the Lord Jesus Christ be with your spirit. Amen" (Phil 4:23).

"The grace of the Lord Jesus Christ be with your spirit" (Philemon 25).

There are several other references in which Paul speaks about his own spirit and how his spirit was refreshed by the spirit of others.

A very important warning.

Be careful to only bless with the words that God wants you to use. It is best to invite the spirit to engage with God and receive from Him what is needed. Be careful not to mix in your own agenda. Don't use this as a manipulative, corrective, or directive tool to try to persuade people to do a certain thing. Become a student of the Bible promises. You can take any scripture that speaks to you and turn it into a blessing.

How do I use this book?

Start by reading the blessings to your own spirit. Allow God to do a deep work in you. Let the blessings speak to your spirit first. Then you will be ready to bless others from the overflow of what He has done in you. The second half of the book is blessings for those around you. Take the words we have written simply as a guide and personalize the blessings for your friends and family.

For more scriptures about your spirit and answers to the most commonly asked questions please see the Appendix starting on page 63. We highly recommend also reading *You Are Blessed In The Names of God* by Sylvia Gunter which contains more teaching on spirit, soul, and body as well as over 100 blessings. This book and other resources are available from www.thefathersbusiness.com.

As you read this book, be blessed as you honor all the gifts that God put in you. May they be released from deep within you with the power of divine grace operating in your whole being. Be blessed to line up and synchronize with the fullness of God's expression in you, so that there is less struggle inside you between spirit, soul, and body. Be blessed inside with clarity, alignment, and harmony. Be blessed in the name of the Creative One who saw all that He had made and called it very good (Gen. 1:31).

© Sylvia Gunter 2017, The Father's Business P.O. Box 380333 Birmingham, AL 35238

Blessings Of Spirit, Soul, And Body

"May God himself, the God of peace, sanctify you through and through. May your whole spirit, soul and body be kept blameless at the coming of our Lord Jesus Christ. The one who calls you is faithful and he will do it" (1 Thess. 5:23-24).

God desires you to be blessed and complete in your spirit, soul, and body. Your human spirit is the innermost part where the Holy Spirit resides.

Spirit, be strengthened through the power of the Holy Spirit (Eph. 3:16). You connect with Him at a deep level. Be blessed with deep calling to deep. If there are areas where you feel crushed or broken, receive the compassion and healing of Jesus who is near to those who are crushed in spirit (Ps. 34:18). May you, spirit, be blessed to receive everything you need to be whole and blameless.

Soul and body, you are valuable and needed. You bring outward expressions of what the spirit feels through words, emotions, and actions. You communicate through smiles, warm embraces, and hands raised in worship. Soul and body, take your place in the dance, allowing your human spirit to lead. Be blessed to partner with the human spirit led by the Holy Spirit.

In areas where you, soul and body, have experienced pain or loss, allow the Holy Spirit working with your spirit to bring transformation and healing. Receive new grace to run the race of life free of weights and entanglements. Your Father is faithful to sanctify every part of you and make you whole. He will do it.

May you receive from Father, Son, and Holy Spirit everything you need each moment. Be blessed as you bring all of who you are into full agreement with all of who He is. Be blessed as the God of peace works to make you complete and whole—spirit, soul, and body.

Your Father's Love

"See what great love the Father has lavished on us, that we should be called children of God! And that is what we are!" (1 John 3:1a).

You are your Beloved's and He is yours (Song 6:3). He called you His beloved from eternity. Your Father was pleased to make you His own (1 Sam. 12:22). The voice of your loving Father resonates in you in a deep place. He is blessing you every day with Himself, nothing less. Your Father wants you to feel His deep attachment to you with cords of never-ending love (Jer. 31:3).

Taste deeply of your Father's love. Hear Him speak to your spirit about your deepest desires and dreams. Know the treasure you are to Him. You are a chosen one, a special person, noticed in your uniqueness, eternally valued. You are priceless and irreplaceable. You are safe in His everlasting embrace, at rest in His non-comparing love. Let your Abba protect you as He surrounds you with the shield of His presence (Ps. 5:12).

Hear Him speak to you about trust and love that is much deeper than the mindset of survival. He says, "Let the beloved of the Lord rest secure in him, for he shields him all day long, and the one the Lord loves rests between his shoulders" (Deu. 33:12).

He is holding you close to Himself. He is whispering to you, "I care for you. I know every detail about you, and wherever you go, I go with you. Wherever you rest, I keep watch. I give you food that will satisfy all your hunger, and I quench all your thirst. I will never hide My face from you. Nothing will ever separate us. Wherever you are, I am." Be blessed by the nearness of your Father who can never leave you or forsake you.

© Sylvia Gunter 2017, The Father's Business P.O. Box 380333 Birmingham, AL 35238

You're A Child Of Father God

"How great is the love the Father has lavished on us, that we should be called children of God! And that is what we are!" (1 John 3:1). *"... God sent the Spirit of his Son into our hearts, the Spirit who calls out, 'Abba, Father.' So you are no longer a slave, but a son; and since you are a son, God has made you also an heir"* (Gal. 4:6-7).

Beloved one, be established in your true identity as a son/daughter of your Father with His blessings as His heir. Be blessed as He reveals to you who you are and affirms to you how He sees you, spotless and blameless in Christ. Deep inside, your heavenly Father calls forth your real essence as His beloved son or daughter. Drink deeply of His lavish love.

May you receive the Spirit of wisdom and revelation, so that you may know God better. May the eyes of your heart be enlightened in order that you may know the hope to which He has called you. Be blessed in the name of your glorious Father who opens the eyes of your heart to know His glorious inheritance and His incomparably great power (Eph. 1:17-19).

Be blessed to receive your heavenly Father calling forth your real value as His beloved. You are a dear member of His family. He marked you with the family likeness of His Son. Be blessed to know Him more richly and love Him more dearly. In Christ you have God's assurance that you are an heir in His Kingdom.

Sealed In Your Father's Pleasure

Your Father recorded in His Word the intention of His pleasure in you. Hear and receive His heart for you in Ephesians 1:5-14 (paraphrased from NLT and personalized for you).

5-6 God's unchanging plan has always been to adopt you into His own family by bringing you to Himself through Jesus Christ. He wanted to do this, and it gave Him great pleasure. So praise Him for His wonderful kindness poured out on you, because you belong to His dearly loved Son.

7-8 God's grace is so rich that He purchased your freedom through the blood of His Son, and your sins are forgiven. He has showered His grace on you, along with all wisdom and understanding.

9-10 God's plan has now been revealed to you; it is a plan centered on Christ, designed long ago according to His good pleasure. At the right time He will bring everything together under the authority of Christ—everything in heaven and on earth.

11-13 Because of Christ, you have received an inheritance from God, for He chose you from the beginning. His purpose was that you who trust in Christ should praise your glorious God. When you believed in Christ, He identified you as His own by giving you the Holy Spirit, whom He promised long ago.

14 Through the Holy Spirit God has marked you as His own. Your inheritance is secure. He did this so you would praise and glorify Him.

This, beloved one, is the pleasure your heavenly Father has in you. Be blessed with being settled in the eternal goodness and kindness of your Father. Be blessed with the seal of His pleasure and glory in His Holy Spirit, guaranteeing your place in your Father's heart.

© Sylvia Gunter 2017, The Father's Business P.O. Box 380333 Birmingham, AL 35238

Your Father's Favor

"For surely, O Lord, you bless the righteous; you surround them with your favor as with a shield" (Ps. 5:12). *"You gave me life and showed me kindness, and in your providence watched over my spirit"* (Job 10:12).

You have the assurance of your Father's presence and surrounding grace. He is your sun and shield, and His honor validates you (Ps. 84:11). Your Abba wants to take you as His precious child next to His heart today. He will keep you close and make His face shine on you and be gracious to you (Num. 6:24-25). Your Father smiles on you with His compassion and His full blessing as you seek Him (Isa. 30:18). He has written this day of your life in His book. You are constantly on His mind (Ps. 139:17-18).

Who you are and everything you have is the result of His favor. Know that your Father sees the path ahead of you, and His providence goes before you to provide for your needs. He is with you to strengthen you and keep you from harm (1 Chron. 4:10). Be blessed as His favor rests on His appointed work through your hands (Ps. 90:17), because His purposes and power for you are great.

Even if circumstances feel hard, be blessed to believe that in those difficult places God is doing you good (Jer. 32:41). His Word says, "The king's heart is in the hand of the Lord; he directs it like a watercourse wherever he pleases" (Pro. 21:1). Be blessed as God breaks through hindrances and uses those around you to fulfill His purpose on your behalf.

He promises that weeping may endure for a night, but joy comes in the morning (Ps. 30:5). He keeps you today in the favor of His love and faithfulness (Pro. 3:3-4).

Awakening

"If Christ is in you, your body is dead because of sin, yet your spirit is alive because of righteousness. And if the Spirit of him who raised Jesus from the dead is living in you, he … will also give life to your mortal bodies through his Spirit, who lives in you" (Rom. 8:10-11).

You are alive in the Spirit of God. God sent His Son into the world, that you might live through Him (1 John 4:9). He has awakened your spirit through His righteousness. He desires your spirit to partner with Him day by day. You are designed to live rejoicing in God.

Paul prayed "that out of his glorious riches he may strengthen you with power through his Spirit in your inner being" (Eph. 3:16). Rise up into all the strength and power God has for you. Your Father intends for you to be strong and enlarged in Him.

Exchange slumber and passivity for the glory of being awakened in Him. The Holy Spirit is present in you, igniting revelation of who you really are. Your spirit is wonderfully designed to do what your soul and body can't do. Be blessed with being active and strong, so that you will be complete spirit, soul, and body (1 Thess. 5:23).

Be blessed to hear your Shepherd when He speaks to you. Be blessed as your spirit leads your soul, directing and instructing it in the ways and will of God's intentions. He knows the "much more" He has for you.

God is up to something significant and eternal in strengthening and enlarging you. Faithfully exercise your God-given identity and authority as a covenant child of God Most High. Be blessed to embrace the abundant life Jesus died to give you.

© Sylvia Gunter 2017, The Father's Business P.O. Box 380333 Birmingham, AL 35238

Identity

"The Spirit you received does not make you slaves, so that you live in fear again; rather, the Spirit you received brought about your adoption to sonship. And by him we cry, 'Abba, Father.' The Spirit himself testifies with our spirit that we are God's children. Now if we are children, then we are heirs—heirs of God and co-heirs with Christ..." (Rom. 8:15-17a).

Be blessed to know your identity as your Father's beloved child. The Holy Spirit assures your spirit that your heavenly Father is yours. He loves you dearly. Be blessed with His tender fathering and receive it as His child. His Spirit speaks to you that you are special to Him.

Jesus grew in wisdom and stature and in favor with God and man. Your Father wants to bless you with growth that is mental, spiritual, emotional, and relational. Let God confirm to you those facets of yourself that He wants to be revealed. Jesus lives in you to shine out of you. Be blessed to grow in character, skills, and potential.

Your Father God delights in how He made you. You are one of His masterpieces. You are His song to be sung in a key of music that is unique to you, in your special rhythm, harmony, and orchestration.

Receive from your Father all the love and acceptance you seek. He wants you to know and enjoy your full identity as His child based purely on relationship, not your performance. Be blessed with perfect love that casts out fear that you aren't enough or don't have what it takes. You are a child of the King, born into His royal family through Christ. You do not have to work for it. It has been freely given to you. You are an heir of the King.

Be blessed to know that your Father is extending His favor to you now. Receive His gift of security in His house. Rest in His grace. Be blessed to live confidently and intentionally in God's heart for you and His purposes for you.

© Sylvia Gunter 2017, The Father's Business P.O. Box 380333 Birmingham, AL 35238

Belonging

"You created my inmost being; you knit me together in my mother's womb. I praise you because I am fearfully and wonderfully made; your works are wonderful, I know that full well. My frame was not hidden from you when I was made in the secret place. When I was woven together in the depths of the earth, your eyes saw my unformed body" (Ps. 139:13-16).

You are very special— handmade and crafted by God your Father. He planned for you before He said, "Let there be light." You are no accident. You did not have to exist—He wanted you. Your life is not a mistake.

God chose the point in time when you were conceived. He chose your mother and your father. He chose every pair of your 23 pairs of chromosomes and every one of your more than 10,000 genes. You are unique, one of a kind. He was pleased when His plans came together as He knit you in your mother's womb. He chose the day and time you would come into the world. He smiled that day. There is nobody else like you.

God celebrates His marvelous design of you. He made your inmost being. You are fearfully and wonderfully made. You are one of His best ideas! You are priceless to Him and deeply loved. You belong to your Abba, the loved child of your perfect heavenly Father. He delights in you. Be blessed to be filled with all His love and joy.

Your heavenly Father affirms you. You have a place in His heart. You are a privilege and a joy. Be blessed with being comfortable in who you are. You are invited to grow into the fullness of who He made you to be. Awaken to the uniqueness of you. Be blessed to be who you were meant to be, living your life in harmony with yourself and with God.

 © Sylvia Gunter 2017, The Father's Business P.O. Box 380333 Birmingham, AL 35238

Worth

"And we all, who with unveiled faces contemplate the Lord's glory, are being transformed into his image with ever-increasing glory, which comes from the Lord, who is the Spirit" (2 Cor. 3:8).

God called you by name and created you to be a reflection of His glory. Be blessed as Jesus is reflected in your life. You are being transformed into His image with ever-increasing glory.

God created you for a purpose. You are an oak of righteousness, a planting of the LORD for the display of His splendor (Isa. 61:3). You were created in Christ Jesus to do good works (Eph. 2:10). Listen to your Father's voice as He speaks your purpose as He sees it. Trust that He will provide all that is needed for you to fulfill His purposes. He has more resources than you can begin to imagine. He has connections to people you haven't met yet.

Be true to the masterpiece that you are. The Lord your Maker crowns you with glory and honor (Isa. 54:5; Ps. 8:5). Never apologize for being who God created you to be. Shine forth your unique display of His image in you.

You have something to give your world that no other person has. Your family and your community need the deposit of Himself that God has placed in your life—"Christ in you, the hope of glory" (Col. 1:27b).

You are of great worth. You are a champion, a treasure. Be blessed as you live from a heart fully alive, being who He made you to be and doing what you were born to do from the inside out.

Intimacy With God

"Then the man and his wife heard the sound of the Lord *God as he was walking in the garden in the cool of the day"* (Gen 3:8).

Welcome God to come into the garden of your heart and fellowship with Him. He wants to walk with you and talk with you, as He did with Adam and Eve. Just be, spending time with Him. Be free of expectation or performance. Allow your Father's heart to minister to your spirit, and respond to Him in adoration.

Be free to know your First Love and to be in harmony with Him. Nothing compares to intimacy with Him. Be bathed in His love and experience His presence. Be blessed in your time with the living God as you are spirit-to-Spirit with Him. God yearns jealously over the spirit that He placed in you (James 4:5). He longs to shine His face upon you and give you peace. Look into His face and experience love, trust, and deep emotional satisfaction in Him.

John 1:14 says, "We have seen his glory, the glory of the One and Only, who came from the Father full of grace and truth." Be blessed to experience the glory of the fullness of grace and truth in Jesus.

God confided in Abraham and Moses. He called them His friends. Christ said to the disciples, "You are My friends." He says to you, "You are my friends if you do what I command. I no longer call you servants, because a servant does not know his master's business. Instead, I have called you friends, for everything that I learned from my Father I have made known to you" (John 15:14-15). You were designed to live in friendship with Him and share your life with Him.

Since friendship is mutual, you give to Him, even as He meets your deepest needs. Be blessed to know Him intimately and pursue Him relentlessly with steadfast hunger for more.

© Sylvia Gunter 2017, The Father's Business P.O. Box 380333 Birmingham, AL 35238

Legitimacy

"Praise be to the God and Father of our Lord Jesus Christ, who has blessed us in the heavenly realms with every spiritual blessing in Christ. For he chose us in him before the creation of the world to be holy and blameless in his sight. In love he predestined us to be adopted as his sons through Jesus Christ, in accordance with his pleasure and will— to the praise of his glorious grace, which he has freely given us in the One he loves" (Eph. 1:3-6).

You existed in God's heart and mind from eternity as a precious being before time was. He chose you. He adopted you as His child through Jesus. He created you for His pleasure, and He delights in you. When God looks at you, He sees the glorious grace of Jesus.

Receive the gentle voice of your Father speaking in the core of your being, "You are my beloved." Be blessed as you live your life as a redeemed child of your Heavenly Father. Allow God to speak to the wounded places in your heart and change the way you see yourself. He wants you to know that you are the apple of His eye, His own special creation (Ps. 17:8).

You have been blessed with every spiritual blessing. God determined for you an appointed place, time, and purpose. In Him you live and move and have your being (Acts 17:26,28). You can trust that today is the day of His favor for you. Stand tall in the truth of who God says you are. Choose to live from His heart for you. Be blessed in Jesus' name as a child of His God and Father.

Sevenfold Blessing

"...the Father, from whom every family in heaven and on earth derives its name" (Eph. 3:14-15).

Spiritual blessings begin with a revelation of God as Abba Father. Be blessed with a love relationship with Him. He wants you to know Jesus personally and grow in Him. Be blessed to desire righteousness that conforms you to the will and ways of God. He wants to give you holy joy in abiding in Him.

Be blessed with emotional blessings. Jesus is your healer of emotions. He releases healing to remove rejection, failure, and shame. Choose forgiveness for yourself and others. Be blessed with peace and joy to replace fear and anxiety (Matt. 10:13) because God never fails. In Him you can have strong hope to believe Him for His promises.

Be blessed with knowing your personal value in Christ. You are of great worth to your heavenly Father. Let Him show you how He sees you in His Son. Receive His favor and His heart for you.

Be blessed with right relationships with others. Let God direct you to right loyalties and wholesome friendships that encourage your life with Him. May you live in healthy community with others.

Be blessed with mental blessing to remove blinders of deception from your mind, so that you will know the truth and have godly wisdom and discernment, knowing good and doing it.

Be blessed with God's health and safety for all physical needs. Lean in to God's strength and protection.

Be blessed in all your labors that God has authored. May your work or studies prosper in the provision of His hands. Acknowledge that He is your source and provider.

I pray blessings. I speak blessings. I choose to be a blessing to you.

© Sylvia Gunter 2017, The Father's Business P.O. Box 380333 Birmingham, AL 35238

Beloved

"I in them and you in me, all being perfected into one. Then the world will know... and will understand that you love them as much as you love me" (John 17:23 NLT).

Your Father said to Jesus at His baptism and at His transfiguration, "You are the Son I love. I am well pleased with You" (Matt. 3:17; 17:5). This was a great affirmation of His love and pleasure in His Son. Because you are in Him, the Father loves you with the same love (John 17:23,26).

Let these words resonate in your spirit. Your Father has deep attachment to you with cords of unfailing love (Jer. 31:3; Hos. 11:4). Hear the voice of your Father speaking deep inside: "You are the beloved." He sees you as a precious person. You are welcome to exist. God celebrates you. Your life is an unceasing "yes" to the truth that you are beloved because of God's great love. In Him you deserve to be valued. That's the truth of your life.

Your Father says, "I called you by name from the very beginning. You belong to Me, and I know you as My own. I am your own true Father. I molded you in your mother's womb. I carved you in the palms of My Son. I hide you in the shadow of My embrace. I care for you tenderly. I count every hair on your head, and wherever you go, I am with you. Wherever you rest, I keep watch. I satisfy all your hunger and quench all your thirst. I will never hide My face from you. Nothing will ever separate us. Wherever you are, I am. Live your life as My redeemed child. You can reach out to true inner freedom and find it ever more fully."

You are accepted in the Beloved (Eph. 1:6 NKJV). You are chosen and you are deeply loved. Say "Yes" to your belovedness. Discover how to fulfill who you are, beloved in God your Father and kept in His Son.

The Light Of God's Face

"In the beginning God created the heavens and the earth. And God said, 'Let there be light,' and there was light. God saw that the light was good, and he separated the light from the darkness" (Gen. 1:1,3-4). *"Every good and perfect gift is from above, coming down from the Father of the heavenly lights, who does not change like shifting shadows"* (James 1:17).

Be blessed in the light of your Father's face. God's voice continually speaks His creative power to your spirit. He gives you good gifts of mercy and peace. Be blessed in His unchanging intention toward you. He gazes at you in rapt attention. Receive long gazes from His countenance. His grace and blessing are in the light of His face toward you (Ps. 67:1).

Join the psalmist's request in Psalm 31:16, "Let your face shine on your servant." Receive the unfailing love of your Father in the light of His eyes. You are your Father's precious one. You belong to His family of light.

He turned you from darkness into His kingdom of light (Col. 1:12-13; Acts 26:18). He makes beauty out of the darkest things. He moves on the turmoil of your life and speaks light in you. Receive His light that lights your way. Receive His purifying light with joy. Receive His light that warms all coldness.

Receive His blessing:

> "The LORD bless you and keep you;
> The LORD make his face shine upon you and be gracious to you;
> The LORD turn his face toward you and give you peace"
> (Num. 6:24-26).

© Sylvia Gunter 2017, The Father's Business P.O. Box 380333 Birmingham, AL 35238

Zephaniah 3:17

"The LORD *your God is with you, he is mighty to save. He will take great delight in you, he will quiet you with his love, he will rejoice over you with singing"* (Zeph. 3:17).

"The LORD *Your God is in the midst of you, a mighty One, a Savior— who saves! He will rejoice over you with joy. He will rest in silent satisfaction... He will exult over you with singing"* (Amplified).

Your Father's heart longs for you. Be blessed as you receive His embrace. He loves you in the way you were created to be loved. He has come to overwhelm you with His love. He takes great delight in you. The prayer of Jesus was "Father, let them know deep inside that as You love Me, so You love them, they in Me and I in You" (John 17:21,26 paraphrased). God loves you as much as He loves His Son. His love for you is way beyond anything you can imagine.

Rest in His presence and let His peace quiet your mind. Let His love calm your heart. He is for you. God is mighty to save. He will fight your battles for you. He has said to you "You will not have to fight this battle. Take up your positions; stand firm and see the deliverance the LORD will give you (2 Chron. 20:17).

Your Father smiles at you today. God likes you — today, every day, every moment. Hear Him rejoicing over you with singing. Let His love be the foundation of your life. You are beloved in the complete finished work of Jesus. God delights in showing you His love.

Let go of the past, as you face the future with your Father. Be blessed with joy, peace, and rest in Him. Be blessed with refreshing and renewal in His presence, as you pursue the fulfillment that He has created for you. Be blessed as He gives you victory and rejoices over you.

Psalm 16

You are kept and protected by God, for He is your refuge. Choose to put your trust in Him and hide yourself in Him.

Be blessed to rejoice in your Lord. You have no good beside or beyond Him.

You are one of the saints of God. You are excellent and glorious. You are a noble one in whom is all of God's delight.

The Lord alone is your chosen and assigned portion and your cup. He holds and maintains your future. Be blessed to rest in His security.

The boundary lines have fallen for you in pleasant places. Surely you have a delightful inheritance.

Be blessed to praise the Lord, who counsels you. Let your spirit receive His instruction even in the night seasons

May you always keep your eyes on the Lord. With God at your right hand, you will not be shaken or moved.

Because of His greatness may your soul be glad and your spirit rejoice. May your body rest and confidently dwell in safety.

Be blessed with assurance that God will not abandon you or let his holy ones see decay.

Be filled with the joy of God's presence. He will make known to you the path of life. At His right hand there are pleasures forevermore.

© Sylvia Gunter 2017, The Father's Business P.O. Box 380333 Birmingham, AL 35238

Ministry Of Jesus

Jesus began His ministry by defining His call and His eternal relationship with you. He said, *"The Spirit of the Lord is on Me, because he anointed me to preach good news to the poor. He has sent me to proclaim freedom for the prisoners and recovery of sight for the blind, to release the oppressed, to proclaim the year of the Lord's favor"* (Luke 4:18-19).

Be blessed to know the mission of Jesus in you now accomplishing His purposes. The resurrection power of Jesus is actively working in you and for you. He wants to do a deep and thorough work in every area of your life.

Hear the good news Jesus brings to you. You are released from slavery. You are liberated from bondages and oppression. Jesus is speaking life to those places that were bruised, crushed, and broken.

Receive new vision to see yourself as God sees you, His favored child. Open your eyes to see the future He is holding for you. God is calling you forth to become the true son/daughter that you are. Embrace this season as the year of God's favor.

Your Father has turned His heart toward you. He is extending His favor to you. The Holy Spirit testifies with your spirit that you are His. He is assuring you of the freedom and full rights you have in Him.

Your Father's favor blesses you every day. You are blessed in the name of the One who favors you for a lifetime (Ps. 30:5). Open wide and receive it. Be blessed with knowing this new place of grace in your Father's favor.

Forgiveness

"If we confess our sins, he is faithful and just and will forgive us our sins and purify us from all unrighteousness" (1 John 1:9). *"As far as the east is from the west, so far has he removed our transgressions from us"* (Ps. 103:12).

Forgiveness brings you close to the heart of God and enlarges your capacity to love. Jesus prayed on the cross, "Father, forgive them; they don't know what they are doing." Be blessed as you look to Jesus and receive healing from any resentment or unforgiveness you carry.

Ask Jesus to help you forgive yourself. He removes your transgressions from you as far as the east is from the west. Feel His cleansing washing over you and making you whole. Be blessed to be released from condemnation, self-judgment, or self-punishment. You are pure and blameless in His sight.

Ask Jesus to help you forgive anyone who has hurt you. Forgiving others doesn't mean that what they did was OK or right. Forgiveness brings complete freedom to your heart and lets God be the judge of all things. Allow God's grace to free you from the bondage of resentment and bitterness.

Ask your Father if you hold any bitterness or anger against Him about what He has allowed in your life. If painful events have distorted your image of God, receive His healing love and compassion. May your spirit and soul see those things from God's point of view through His spiritual insight and understanding (Col. 1).

May the grace of God do the deep work of forgiveness in you. The Lord says though your sins are like scarlet, they shall be as white as snow; though they are red as crimson, they shall be like wool (Isa. 1:18). Be blessed to choose to live from that freedom. Be blessed in the name of Jesus who paid the complete price for sin.

 © Sylvia Gunter 2017, The Father's Business P.O. Box 380333 Birmingham, AL 35238

Abandonment

"You brought me out of the womb; you made me trust in you even at my mother's breast. From birth I have relied on you... I will ever praise you" (Ps. 22:9; Ps. 71:6).

For every relationship or circumstance that made you feel unwanted or unloved, God is there for you. Jesus invites you to give Him all your wounded places in exchange for His unconditional love and grace. Be blessed as you release to Him all of the pain you are carrying. Jesus was wounded so that you may be healed (Isa. 53:5).

Allow God to fill up the holes in your heart that crave affirmation and connection. Ask God to come into your deepest needs and show you who He is for you in those places. Receive healing from Him as He binds you to Himself with cords that cannot be broken.

God is a most caring and compassionate Father. You are a precious one to be protected, nurtured, and honored. His grace and gentleness heals all wounds that you received from the words and actions of others. The God of all mercy cleanses all feelings that He didn't author. Feel His living water wash over you, making you pure and complete.

Receive God's blessing in your inmost being. He will restore the years the locusts have eaten. Be blessed to continue to receive the ministry of your Abba Father. In His time He will repair every place where trust was broken. He finishes what He begins.

Be strong to embrace life as God intends for you. Understand that you are loved, cared for, and significant. You give Him joy. Settle down in the safety of your Heavenly Father's embrace. Rest in His love. He is always there for you.

God Can Re-parent You

"And the God of all grace, who called you to his eternal glory in Christ, after you have suffered a little while, will himself restore you and make you strong, firm and steadfast" (1 Peter 5:10).

God desires for mothers and fathers to be an example of His love. As you look back on your life, it may be hard to hear that God is a loving Father. Even if you had a good family, no parents are perfect. Their best intentions may have missed the mark. Your Heavenly Father wants to re-parent you. He can heal the wounded places. He will restore you and make you strong, firm and steadfast.

God called Himself "the Father of our spirit" (Heb. 12:9b). May your Father speak deeply to your spirit. He has put His name on you and blessed you (Num. 6:27). You are valued and cherished by your Father. You are a treasure to Him. Be blessed to believe that He never stops being your dear tender Abba full of mercy and compassion. You are always His pleasure as the child He uniquely created to love.

Be blessed to receive perfect love from your Abba Father today and every day. Let Him re-Father you in true biblical sonship. Be blessed with life-changing encounters with His Father-heart for you. Receive His deep healing work that restores your spirit and soul. God can heal you to wholeness.

Settle down in your Abba's love. Receive His kind intention toward you. Soak in His matchless love for you. Allow Him to show you what your true Father is like. He is strong. He is kind. He is caring. He is near and attentive. He is for you. He will never leave you.

You can lean on His mercy and compassion. You always have His blessing. You are safe and secure in His provision.

Your Father is inviting you to connect deeply with Him. Be blessed with new freedom of spirit in Him, unhindered and holy. Awake to life as the joyful child of the King that He created you to be.

 © Sylvia Gunter 2017, The Father's Business P.O. Box 380333 Birmingham, AL 35238

Physical Healing

"The power of Jesus was present for him to heal the sick" (Luke 5:17). *"Jesus Christ is the same yesterday, and today, and forever"* (Heb 13:8).

You belong to your Abba, the King of creation. He takes care of what is His and has compassion on all He has made. God is the Father of mercies and God of all comfort (2 Cor. 1:3-4). Your Father hears your prayers and tears of pain. Receive His heart toward you.

While on earth Jesus compassionately ministered to those who needed healing (Matt. 14:14). His touch is as powerful as when He walked on the earth. His love for you is steadfast, and His compassion never fails. Jesus is your healing and wholeness.

He who raised Jesus from the dead will also give life to your mortal body through His Spirit who lives in you (Rom. 8:11). Invite your spirit to partner with the Holy Spirit as He ministers to your body. Be blessed as the healing of Jesus flows to every cell, bringing every part of your body into God's alignment.

Be blessed with faith to believe that Jesus has authority over sickness and death. His resurrection power is present for you to be healed and whole. Come boldly to the throne of our gracious God, so that your body may receive His mercy for healing.

Allow the Living Water to wash from your spirit, soul, and body anything that is not of God. May the love and power of your Jehovah Rapha fill you completely.

As you wait patiently for God's ultimate healing, rest in God's perfect love that casts out fear. Hear Jesus speaking "Peace, be still" to all your worries and fears. You are in His hands. He is with you. He will strengthen you and help you. He will uphold you by His righteous right hand (Isa. 41:10).

Hope In Disappointment

"I am the Lord; those who hope in me will not be disappointed" (Isa. 49:23b). *"Be joyful in hope, patient in affliction, faithful in prayer"* (Rom. 12:12).

God created everything to work together in perfect harmony. Sadly, our broken world is full of disappointments. Nothing on earth (circumstances, people, hopes, and dreams) works as they were designed by God in the beginning. Your spirit longs for all things to be restored where there will be no more sorrow.

When life hasn't turned out like you expected and you feel let down, Jesus understands. He was called a man of sorrows (Isa. 53:3). He is acquainted with every feeling you are experiencing. Bring Him all your disappointments.

Be blessed with rest in God alone when your expectation is delayed. Be blessed with unshakable hope in Him, when everything is shaken. The Lord promises that those who wait and hope expectantly in Him will not be disappointed or put to shame.

Hebrews 6:18-19 says, "We have this hope as an anchor for the soul, firm and secure." Confidently take hold of God's character, His unchangeableness, and His promises. Your Father will never change His mind about you. Be blessed as you receive His hope as the strong and trustworthy anchor of your soul.

Your Father is God of everything, even your challenges and trials. He knows the mysteries of your life. Be blessed with hope as God washes away disappointments with new vision and renewed expectation. Receive His touch to restore the places that have been bruised, broken, and shut down. Allow Him to replace your burdens with His faith, your disappointments with His hope, and your doubts with His love

Be blessed as the God of hope fills you with His joy and peace. (Rom. 15:13).

 © Sylvia Gunter 2017, The Father's Business P.O. Box 380333 Birmingham, AL 35238

Comfort For Those Who Mourn

"The Spirit of the Sovereign Lord is on me, because the Lord has anointed me... He has sent me to bind up the brokenhearted ... to comfort all who mourn, and provide for those who grieve in Zion— to bestow on them a crown of beauty instead of ashes, the oil of gladness instead of mourning, and a garment of praise instead of a spirit of despair" (Isa. 61:1-3).

Your Heavenly Father is faithful to comfort you in your grief. These days may not feel like His goodness or His faithfulness. Be blessed to trust that God is good and kind even if it doesn't feel like it in this moment. Hear His gentle invitation to come to Him and receive His love, comfort, and guidance. The indwelling Christ is anointed in your life to bring good news to you, to bind up your broken heart.

He hears your prayers and your tears when there are no words. He counts them as liquid intercession, which is precious to Him (Ps. 56:8a). Be blessed to know Him as your Father of compassion and God of all comfort, who comforts you in all your troubles (2 Cor. 1:3-4). Receive the covering of His sweet presence and peace that passes all understanding.

Be blessed with strength and courage as you face the days ahead. You are not alone. He is your Mighty Warrior who contends with those forces that are contending with you (Isa. 42:13; Ps. 35:1). May you be at peace with a still heart, while He fights for you (Exo. 14:14; Ps. 46:10).

Be blessed in His covenant of love that can never be taken from you (Rom. 8:35,38-39). He will never leave you. His promises can never be broken. He never loses sight of who He created you uniquely to be. Bring Him your grief and pain as often as you need to and receive His crown of beauty and oil of gladness. Allow Him to heal all your wounded places and restore you with His love. He is more than enough for your every need.

Healing From Trauma

"'For I know the plans I have for you,' says the Lord. 'They are plans for good and not for disaster, to give you a future and a hope... I will be found by you,' says the Lord. 'I will end your captivity and restore your fortunes'" (Jer. 29:11,14.)

Sometimes there are events that are too difficult to process. When trauma occurs, your spirit, soul, and body are all effected in different ways. You can feel overwhelmed and unable to cope. Be blessed to know there is a Healer who is full of compassion toward you. Jesus understands what it means to be deeply troubled.

Be blessed in your spirit, soul, and body to know and understand full healing and freedom in Jesus. He binds up the brokenhearted. He proclaims freedom for captives and release from darkness for prisoners (Isa. 61). Jesus is here to release you from all fear and anxiety that is affecting your spirit, soul, and body.

May your spirit hear from the Father what is needed to comfort your soul and heal your body. If you feel captive because of wounding, be blessed with His love and power to release you into His freedom. May your soul be in the present with the I AM, not going back to pain of the past or running ahead to the "what if's" of the future. Be released from holding onto anything that Jesus didn't give you.

Body, be free to release all effects of fear, anxiety, worry, and stress. Allow Jesus to take everything He did not design your body to carry. By His wounds you are healed. Be blessed in your memory that is holding on to trauma. Be blessed as God restores healthy connections in your brain. Receive His healing grace in everything that is out of His order.

God's thoughts toward you are for peace. His plans for you are healing and restoration. God told Hezekiah, "I have heard your prayer, I have seen your tears, I will heal you" (2 Kings 20:5). That's quite a promise, and it is as true today as when it was spoken.

© Sylvia Gunter 2017, The Father's Business P.O. Box 380333 Birmingham, AL 35238

Blessing Of A New Name

"I will write on him, the name of my God…and I will also write on him my new name" (Rev. 3.12). "You will be called by a new name that the mouth of the LORD will bestow. No longer will they call you Deserted, or name your land Desolate... for the LORD will take delight in you, and your land will be married" (Isa. 62:2,4).

The words and actions of others may cause you to believe negative things about yourself. You may carry false labels and names. Receive the compassion of Jesus to address this pain. Allow God to wash away anything that He did not author. Receive His healing grace in everything that is out of God's order.

Your Father blesses you with purity, holiness, and cleansing. He can re-innocence you. He wants to, so let Him. Feel the cleansing of the Living Water washing you and making you whole. Be blessed to be released from condemnation, self-judgment, or self-punishment. You are pure and blameless in His sight. There is no spot or blemish on you.

Be blessed to hear God say "Fear not, for I have redeemed you; I have called you by name, you are mine" (Isa. 43:1). Your heavenly Father is writing His name on you. Ask Him to give you His new name for you, a term of endearment, or a picture of how He see you. Be blessed to receive His words of life, hope, and goodness that He speaks to you.

Be blessed with new openness to people, to life, and to God. Be blessed with confidence and anticipation of a future filled with hope. You are a beloved child of the King. You have honor, dignity, and worth in Christ. He will make your righteous reward shine like the dawn, your vindication like the noonday sun (Ps. 37:6).

His power has given you everything you need for life and godliness. He has given you His very great and precious promises (2 Peter 1:3-4). He is able to keep you from stumbling and to present you before His glorious presence without fault and with great joy (Jude 24).

Comfort: His Holy Exchange

Jesus quoted Isaiah 61, in which God promises His Messiah would give a holy exchange: comfort for grief, a crown instead of ashes, gladness for mourning, and praise instead of despair (Luke 4:18-19). *Then Jesus said, "Today this scripture is fulfilled in your hearing"* (Luke 4:21).

Your Comforter knows your grief, your ashes, your mourning and despair. He longs to take these from you and give you His compassion and grace. God is ministering Himself to you by His Spirit. Your Father of mercy speaks tenderly to you. The resurrection power of Jesus is more powerful than the wounds, unforgiveness, and grief that erect walls in parts of your heart. He can make new life sprout from barren places. The Holy Spirit produces peace, the joy of the Lord, and hope in Him that transcends your circumstances.

Be blessed to know the One who comforts you as a mother comforts her child (Isa. 66:13). Receive His holy exchange: comfort for grief, a crown instead of ashes, gladness for mourning, and praise instead of despair. Rest in the love, covenant mercy, and faithfulness of your Father. Jesus, who walked on the waters, is present in your turbulence and storms, saying, "Peace, be still." Be blessed as you take refuge in the strong arms of the Prince of Peace.

God is still on His throne as the ruling Lord and King. He remains faithful to you. He is tender in His compassion toward you. He is your consolation. He made a covenant of grace with you, and He cannot break His covenant. His promises are sure, His presence cannot leave you.

 © Sylvia Gunter 2017, The Father's Business P.O. Box 380333 Birmingham, AL 35238

Trust

"Why are you downcast, Oh my soul? Why so disturbed within me? Put your hope in God, for I will yet praise him, my Savior and my God" (Ps. 43:5). *"But I trust in your unfailing love; my heart rejoices in your salvation. I will sing to the LORD, for he has been good to me"* (Ps. 13:5-6).

When things are hard and you don't understand, be blessed to lift up your head and allow God's face to shine upon you and receive His peace (Num. 6:25). Nothing takes Him by surprise. He knows the end from the beginning (Isa. 46:9-10). He will never leave you or forsake you. His is with you, a very present help (Heb. 13:5–6; Ps. 46:1).

God is the God of all comfort, your Father of mercies (2 Cor. 1:3–4). Feel His tender heart reaching out to you. He is inviting you to climb up in His lap and find comfort there. He has a heart that tears can touch (Ps. 56:8). Be blessed to bring God all your questions. Pour out your heart to Him. He is your loving Father, full of compassion. He is here for you. If it matters to you, it matters to Him. He cares for you.

Your earthly relationships may have hurt your ability to trust. Allow God to heal your broken truster. He is near the brokenhearted. Like the Psalmist, choose to trust in God's unfailing love in spite of your circumstances. Ask God to give you a song to sing in the dark times (Ps. 13).

When answers feel delayed or when disappointment tries to overwhelm you, lean into His abundant grace that is more than enough for your every need. Be blessed to trust there is no circumstance or person that the blood of Jesus does not cover.

Trust that He will give gladness instead of mourning and praise instead of fainting. Weeping may endure for a night, but He gives joy in the morning (Isa. 61:3; Ps. 30:5).

Overcomer's Blessing

"'I pray also that the eyes of your heart may be enlightened in order that you may know … his incomparably great power for us who believe. That power is like the working of his mighty strength, which he exerted in Christ when he raised him from the dead and seated him at his right hand in the heavenly realms" (Eph. 1:18-20).

You are identified with the death, burial, and resurrection of Jesus. You live in the risen and ascended Christ every day because God raised you up with Him. He is your life in all His resurrection power (Phil. 3:10).

Because of what Christ did, you are hidden in God and sealed by the power of the Holy Spirit. Choose to live from the reality of the finished work of Christ's resurrection and ascension. All authority in heaven and on earth has been given to Jesus, and you are seated with Him at the right hand of the Father, established in His authority (Eph. 2:6). You live in His power and dominion over spiritual forces of darkness. You reign in life through Christ.

Be blessed to understand your true position in Christ. The Spirit of Christ Jesus is present every day in you so that you can live always from your spirit, not allowing the soul or body to take over.

You are a covenant child of God Most High. He is the God of all grace, God of the impossible. You have the privilege of coming into agreement with Him in your spirit, soul, and body. You are intended to live in honor and authority in Jesus' name. You are on kingdom business. Be blessed to represent your King everywhere you go.

© Sylvia Gunter 2017, The Father's Business P.O. Box 380333 Birmingham, AL 35238

Peace

"Gideon built an altar to the LORD there and called it The LORD is Peace" (Judges 6:24). *"I will listen to what God the LORD says; he promises peace to his people, his faithful servants"* (Ps. 85:8). *"For he himself is our peace"* (Eph. 2:14).

Jehovah-shalom is one of the covenant names by which God has bound Himself to you. Shalom means completeness, harmony, and fulfillment. Be blessed with full assurance that everything is all right because God has everything under His care. Jesus in you, your Prince of peace, means that you are settled and at rest in unworried blessedness even in the midst of life's storms.

Be blessed to know the healing power of His presence and His restoration of every broken place. His mighty power gives you victory over every enemy. Be blessed with unshakable faith to believe His sufficiency meets every need that you face through His limitless resources.

God's covenant of peace is more than just the absence of struggle and fear. His peace is for your security and well-being. Receive the blessing of shalom from your covenant-keeping God. He is the government of peace in your life. His peace gives you safety, joy, and wholeness of your spirit, soul, and body.

Be blessed in Him, your true shalom. He alone is your complete and total fulfillment. Be blessed with God's unshakable peace from the inside out. Be blessed with harmony of spirit, soul, and body. Be blessed with the benefits of His covenant of peace in harmony with yourself, with God, and with others. Be blessed with His peace as your covering, so your heart knows Him in His fullness.

Psalm 91

Your life is lived in great spiritual warfare, but you are sheltered in the safe refuge of the Almighty. Be at home in the hiding place of Most High. Rest under His wings (1). He is the Lord, your refuge and fortress. You are defended by His faithfulness as your shield and defense (2).

Be blessed with security from satan's snares and schemes (3). You have peace in El Shaddai. His promises are sure (4). God hears your heart's cry. Be blessed to put into God's hands the terrors in the dark and the arrows that attempt to destroy you by day (5-6).

Stand steadfast in your Commander of the Lord's hosts. See that the battle is the Lord's. No weapon formed against you will prosper (7-8). You have the Author and Finisher of faith in you to enable you to trust the unfailing protection of God Most High. He is your hope and trust, your true home (9).

Jesus in you stands against all hindrances. You have His name and the authority of His blood, the cross, resurrection, and ascension. He has already defeated the adversary you are facing. In His name you have victory (10). God is the Commander of the armies of heaven. He will command His angels to guard you. His angels will hold you up so you don't stumble (11-12).

Jesus has already defeated every foe. You have nothing to fear. Stand as a covenant child of God Most High. Be bold, be free, and take your rightful authority in your protector (13).

God promises to rescue you because you love Him (14). He will pay attention to you and be with you in trouble. He promises to deliver you and give you the honor due you as the object of His strong care (15). His crowning promise is that He will fill you with the satisfaction of a full life and show you His victory. In Him you will be truly satisfied (16).

© Sylvia Gunter 2017, The Father's Business P.O. Box 380333 Birmingham, AL 35238

Direction

"I will instruct you and teach you in the way you should go; I will counsel you with my loving eye on you" (Ps. 32:8).

Your life is like a treasure map, and you are on a journey of discovery. As you follow after God you will see that it is not a specific destination that is most important. Each stop along the way is created by God to show you more of Himself.

Be blessed as you follow His faithful guidance. He will teach you His ways and make you sensitive to His hand on your life. Be blessed with assurance that you don't go anywhere today without your personal Guide. Be blessed with His open door before you that no one can shut, according to His sovereign will, and with closed doors that are outside His purposes for you (Rev. 3:7-8). May the blessing of His presence lead your spirit.

Wherever you go, God promises "Whether you turn to the right or to the left, your ears will hear a voice behind you, saying, 'This is the way; walk in it'" (Isa. 30:21). Be blessed as you hear Him whisper direction, "This is the way. Walk this way." If His word is to fight, let it be for His glory. If He says to wait, let it be with hope and grace, secure in His timing and sovereign hand. If His word is to flee, let it be with His permission and at His direction. If He tells you to offer a sacrifice of praise, let it be with thanksgiving that is sweet to Him.

Be blessed to be confident that He is working out all things for good, whether you see it or feel it now. His eyes are open to all your ways (Jer. 32:19). Let your expectation be centered in Him (Ps. 62:1,5). Receive His peace as He directs your paths. He promises that He will keep in perfect peace those whose eyes are fixed on Him, because you trust in Him (Isa. 26:3).

Refreshment

"Those who hope in the LORD will renew their strength. They will soar on wings like eagles; they will run and not grow weary, they will walk and not be faint" (Isa. 40:31). *"For with you is the fountain of life"* (Ps. 36:9).

When you feel exhausted and at the end of your endurance, receive God's holy strength and refreshment. Psalm 107:35 says, "He turned the desert into pools of water and the parched ground into flowing springs." When you're in a wilderness, be blessed to drink from waters that stream from the hard places because He is your Spiritual Rock (1 Cor. 10:4).

Isaiah 49:10 says that His compassion will guide you and lead you beside springs of water. God will make the Valley of Trouble into a place of springs, and you will go from strength to strength in Him (Ps. 84:6).

God committed Himself to you as your Abba, and He will meet all your needs today. You will not lack any good thing (Ps. 84:11). He has covenanted to heal and strengthen you. Be still inside, look to Him, and receive the power of the Holy Spirit. Let Him re-fill and rejuvenate you.

Be blessed to receive your Abba's love in all its fullness. Receive His Spirit of wisdom and understanding, so that you take only His yoke upon you. His yoke is easy and His burden is light (Matt. 11:28-30). You can be confident in His ability and presence at work in your life in everything that concerns you. You have His favor and blessing as a shield.

God gives you grace for today. Tomorrow He will greet you with a whole new supply of Himself. Be blessed with peace and security in Him. Receive His sweet presence each moment.

 © Sylvia Gunter 2017, The Father's Business P.O. Box 380333 Birmingham, AL 35238

Favor

"For surely, O LORD, you bless the righteous; you surround them with your favor as with a shield" (Ps. 5:12).

Who you are and everything you have is the result of God's favor. He has blessed you with every spiritual blessing (Eph. 1:3). You are surrounded by His grace.

Your Abba wants to take you as His precious child right up next to His heart today. He will keep you close and make His face shine on you and be gracious to you (Num. 6:24-25). Your Father smiles on you with His compassion as you seek Him (Isa. 30:18).

Your Father's providence goes before you to provide for every need. He is with you to strengthen you and keep you from harm (1 Chron. 4:10). The LORD God is a sun and shield; He bestows favor and honor; no good thing does He withhold (Ps. 84:11).

He has written this day of your life in His book. Be blessed as His favor rests on His appointed work through your hands (Ps. 90:17). See the great thing He is about to do (1 Sam. 12:6). His Word says, "The king's heart is in the hand of the LORD; he directs it like a watercourse wherever he pleases" (Pro. 21:1). Be blessed as God breaks through hindrances and uses everything to fulfill His purposes. He rejoices today in doing you good (Jer. 32:41).

Even if circumstances make it hard to believe, trust in His unfailing love. He is not slow in keeping His promise. He surrounds you with the shield of His presence (Ps. 5:12). He promises that weeping may endure for a night, and His anger is only for a moment. Joy comes in the morning, and His favor lasts for your lifetime (Ps. 30:5). He keeps you today in His love and faithfulness (Pro. 3:3-4). He is inviting you to live in the assurance of your Father's blessing and favor. Be blessed to trust His goodness toward you today.

Morning Blessing

"This is the day that You have made. I will rejoice and be glad in it" (Ps. 118:24).

Be blessed with waking up each morning refreshed and greatly anticipating another new day in communion with your Father, your Redeemer, your Friend. He awakens you morning by morning, and He is eager to speak to you (Isa. 50:4). Let God minister Himself to you. Be blessed to hear His words of love spoken specifically to you. Each day the Lord pours out His unfailing love to you. Receive His steadfast love and His mercies that are new for you today. You have everything you need for life and godliness.

As you start this new day, allow your spirit partnering with the Holy Spirit to take the lead over your soul and body. Choose to align your spirit, soul, and body with Father, Son, and Holy Spirit in complete agreement.

Regardless of what the day brings, be blessed to anchor yourself in God. He is your rock and fortress. He is your shield and strong tower. He is enthroned in every circumstance and relationship. The Lord will guard your going out and your coming in (Ps. 121:8). He is always there for you.

Actively bless every place where you go with the presence of God Most High. By His presence in you, be blessed as you carry the holy blessing of cleansing and restoration in Jesus' name. Be blessed in the name of the Presence who lives in you (Exo. 33:14).

© Sylvia Gunter 2017, The Father's Business P.O. Box 380333 Birmingham, AL 35238

Evening Blessing

*"The L*ORD *will go before you, the God of Israel will be your rear guard"* (Isa. 52:12). *"Have you not put a hedge around him and his household and everything he has?"* (Job 1:10).

At the end of your day, allow God to wash away from you anything not of Him that He does not intend for you to carry. Be blessed with God's mercy and grace. You are clothed in the righteousness of the Lamb of God and anointed with the oil of His Spirit.

God has sovereign control over all things. Trust that He knows what is best for you and what will bring Him the most glory. Present to God on open palms everyone and everything that concerns you. Trust Him to be the protector of your family, your possessions, everything in your physical and spiritual jurisdiction.

Rejoice in your Redeemer who is faithful and true. The Captain of the Lord's hosts fights for you. He sends His mighty angels to surround you. Through the blood of Jesus He dismisses all enemy assignments and protects you from harm (Ps. 91).

Be blessed to rest secure in Him. He has placed a holy hedge around you and your household. Invite God to fill your household with His Holy Spirit.

The LORD promises that His presence will go with you, and He will give you rest (Exo. 33:14). Be blessed to nestle into the Spirit to let Him work in the deepest part of you while you sleep. He will counsel you and speak to you in the night (Ps. 16:7). Your spirit can rest and receive downloads of everything that you need from His presence.

Be blessed with being enriched in communing with Him in the night seasons. Receive the grace of the presence of the Lord with you and the release of His blessing of presence around you.

Night Watch Blessing

"I will praise the Lord, who counsels me;
even at night my heart instructs me" (Ps. 16:7).

"By day the Lord directs his love, at night his song is with me—
a prayer to the God of my life" (Ps. 42:8).

"I remembered my songs in the night.
My heart meditated and my spirit inquired" (Ps. 77:6).

Spirit, while I am asleep tonight, keep your eyes on the Father. Receive His download for tomorrow that He has provided for me, which Jesus purchased on the cross.

Soul, dial down. My human spirit is in control, led by the Holy Spirit. You are valuable and irreplaceable, but you are not in charge. I bind my mind to the mind of Christ. In Jesus' name, I close every file in my mind the enemy inserted or reopened today. I bind my will to the Father's will. I bind my emotions to the Holy Spirit for healing and alignment.

Body, take your proper position under my spirit by the Holy Spirit. Line up everything that needs to be healed by the blood of Jesus, and receive your healing.

Father, I submit myself to you. I am sleeping in your arms. Thank You, Father, that it is Your will for me to be complete—spirit, soul, and body. I can count on You to do this, because "The one who called you is faithful and He will do it" (1 Thess. 5:23-24).

© Sylvia Gunter 2017, The Father's Business P.O. Box 380333 Birmingham, AL 35238

Wedding

"And the two will become one flesh. So they are no longer two, but one flesh" (Mark 10:8).

Each of you is a unique image-bearer of your loving Father. You are both a product of His love. You bear His craftsmanship. There is no one else in the world like you. Be blessed to live in the freedom of how He made each of you to be.

As you enter marriage, you remain the incredible creations that God intended for His glory. At the same time you become one. You are creating your own identity separate from your families. Be blessed to have the courage to explore this mystery of marriage. God created you to be a blessing and a treasure to each other. Be blessed to grow toward one another with God's heart as you love each other well.

Precious wife, be a lifelong student of your husband. Be blessed to learn his spirit, soul, and body. Be blessed to make home a safe place. Through your words and actions invite him to be the man he was created to be. As his beautiful wife, you are his ideal partner, according to Genesis 2:18. God has uniquely blessed you to walk alongside him as his companion in gentleness and grace. You are revealing aspects of God's character that only you can reveal.

Precious husband, love your wife, as Christ loved the church. This is easier to say than to do. Be blessed with wisdom from the Father as you love her well. Listen to her heart. Delight in the beauty of who she is both inside and out. Give her a safe place to express her inmost thoughts and emotions. As her husband, you reveal facets of God's character that she would otherwise never know. The best you can give is to offer her Christ living in you.

You have been blessed with family and friends who love and support you. God is your biggest fan and best cheerleader. Stay close to Him as He guides you in your marriage. Cling to His love that was revealed on the cross, and release His love to one another as you walk this journey together.

© Sylvia Gunter 2017, The Father's Business P.O. Box 380333 Birmingham, AL 35238

Marriage

In Genesis 2:18 God said it is not good for a man to be alone, and He would create an ideal helper fit for him. The literal translations from the Hebrew is "according to the opposite of him, an ideal match." Husband and wife, God created each of you as unique individuals. You each reflect the nature of God in your own special way. You are intended to fill in each other's gaps so that the sum of your union is greater than the parts.

Be blessed to celebrate each other's strengths rather than focusing on each other's weaknesses. Be blessed as God deepens and develops your character. Be blessed with patience and grace toward each other. Iron will sharpen iron as you grow together in Him.

Husband, rejoice in your wife. Be blessed to prize her and love her as Christ loves His bride, the church. Be filled with God's love that teaches you how to nurture and cherish her (Eph. 5:28-29).

Wife, be filled with God's love for your husband. Be blessed to notice him, regard him, respect him, and admire him (Eph. 5:33, Amplified). May your tender embrace satisfy him. May your love alone fill him with delight (Pro. 5:19).

Be blessed to walk together in Jesus so you can have fellowship of spirit with each other (1 John 1:7). Be blessed to honor God by submitting to one another (Eph. 5:21). Live at peace in perfect union by loving, honoring, and respecting one another (1 Thess. 5:13). Be quick to forgive each other. In so doing you model God's extravagant grace. Be vigilant to guard against any separation of spirit between the two of you.

Receive God's mercies that are new every morning so that your lovingkindness for each other may be renewed. May you go through life together as friends and lovers, husband and wife, and servants of God.

 © Sylvia Gunter 2017, The Father's Business P.O. Box 380333 Birmingham, AL 35238

Wife

"The king is enthralled by your beauty; honor him, for he is your lord. All glorious is the princess within her chamber; her gown is interwoven with gold" (Ps. 45:11,13).

Beloved wife, be blessed to see yourself as God sees you. You are a glorious princess, and the King is enthralled with your beauty. He is captivated by you. You are a delight.

Hear your Beloved say to you "My dove in the clefts of the rock, in the hiding places on the mountainside, show me your face, let me hear your voice; for your voice is sweet, and your face is lovely" (Song 2:14). As much as I want to be a safe place for you, God is your true refuge. He is your shelter and high tower. Be blessed to share with Him your inmost hurts, hopes, and dreams. He is always here for you.

As my precious wife, you are my ideal partner (Gen. 2:18) as you reveal the gentleness and grace of God. You are showing aspects of God's character that only a wife can. You are blessed with inner beauty that never fades, the eternal youth that is found in holding fast to the things that never age. You are a wife of noble character who is my crown (Pro. 12:5).

May the peace of God rule your heart (Col. 3:15). Be blessed to trust in God with all your heart, not depending on your own understanding, but acknowledging Him in all your ways (Prov. 3:5-6). May Christ be more at home in your heart day by day. May your roots go down deep into God's marvelous love. May you feel and understand how long, how wide, how deep, and how high His love is for you.

Husband

"And a voice from heaven said, 'This is my Son, whom I love; with him I am well pleased'" (Matt. 3:17).

Beloved husband, be blessed to see yourself as God sees you. You are a son who pleases Him. He delights in how He made you. You are a unique display of His heart and character.

May you have the rich experience of knowing Christ with certainty. God's plan for you is Christ Himself (Col. 2:2-3). Be blessed with the mind of Christ, saturated with godly wisdom (James 3:17). May you take every thought captive (1 Cor. 2:16).

Be blessed to trust in God with all your heart, not depending on your own understanding, but acknowledging Him in all your ways (Pro. 3:5-6). May the favor of the Lord rest on you. May God bless and establish the work of your hands and heart (Ps. 90:17).

The man who trusts in the Lord and whose hope is in Him is blessed (Jer. 17:7). Be blessed to know that God is your arm every morning and your salvation in times of trouble (Isa. 33:2). He is always with you. You have everything you need to succeed because He is for you.

May the peace of God rule your heart (Col. 3:15). May Christ be more at home in your heart day by day. May your roots go down deep into God's marvelous love. May you feel and understand how long, how wide, how deep, and how high God's love is for you.

As my loving husband, you are my ideal partner (Gen. 2:18). God has uniquely blessed us to walk alongside each other as companions. Be blessed as you rejoice in me. Prize me and love me as Christ loves His bride, the church. (Eph. 5:28-29). May we be blessed with wisdom from the Father who shows us how to nurture and cherish each other. You are revealing aspects of God's character that only a husband can. You reflect God's strength, faithful care, and protection through your words and actions. I am honored to be your wife.

 © Sylvia Gunter 2017, The Father's Business P.O. Box 380333 Birmingham, AL 35238

Mom-And-Dad-To-Be

"Children are a heritage from the LORD, offspring a reward from him" (Ps. 127:3).

Mom-and-Dad-to-be, be filled with joy as you celebrate the precious gift God is giving you. With tender care He chose to knit your baby together. He is singing over this little unborn one with songs of joy (Zeph. 3:17). Be blessed to be wise stewards of this gift. May you reflect God's gracious love and care.

The weight of being a parent can feel overwhelming. Be blessed with God's perfect love that takes away all fear. Allow God to quiet your minds. Be blessed with peace in your parenting, because you are mentored by the Lord of peace Himself. God's hands are on all circumstances in your life. Every situation will be a learning opportunity, as His Spirit guides and equips you to parent.

God is intimately acquainted with your child. God knew your baby before you knew you were pregnant. He has been watching over your child's spirit from the beginning (Job 10:12). God is the author of all life. Every day of your baby's life is written in His book. Be blessed to keep your own spirit in tune with God's spirit so that you may shepherd your child's heart well. Be blessed to release all your expectations and welcome with open arms the one God has made. May God fill you with the knowledge of His will through all spiritual wisdom and understanding (Col. 1:9).

God shows His love to a thousand generations of those who love Him and keep His commandments. Be blessed to draw on the deep reservoir of your spiritual legacy from godly ancestors in past generations. May your own love relationships with God be so captivating that your child is drawn to Jesus. Be blessed to create your own legacy by praising God's works and declaring His mighty acts to the next generation (Ps. 145:4).

Baby

"I praise you because I am fearfully and wonderfully made; your works are wonderful, I know that full well. My frame was not hidden from you when I was made in the secret place, when I was woven together in the depths of the earth. Your eyes saw my unformed body; all the days ordained for me were written in your book before one of them came to be" (Ps. 139:14-16).

Precious little one, God created you spirit, soul, and body in your mother's womb. Since the day He placed you there, He has watched over your spirit with His perfect love and care. God knew you before your Mom knew you existed. He has been with you since the beginning. When He created the universe, you were on His mind (Eph. 1:4). At the perfect time He has caused you to be born. You are loved with an everlasting love by a perfect heavenly Father. Hear the song that your Father rejoices to sing over you (Zeph. 3:17).

God celebrates His marvelous design of you. Every detail of your spirit, soul, and body are a result of God's intentional thoughts. As you grow through the stages and seasons of your life, be blessed to be secure and comfortable in who God has made you to be. God likes the way He made you.

God is the author of all life. Every day of your life is written in His book. Be blessed to know that your Father has a purpose for you. His ultimate purpose is that you may know Him and the power of His resurrection (Phil. 3:10).

God knows the plans He has for you. These plans will give you hope and a future. Be blessed to be who God has created you to be. Pursue the good works which God has prepared in advance for you to do (Eph. 2:10).

Be blessed with hunger for spiritual things so that you respond to Jesus' invitation to eternal life. May you grow in the grace and knowledge of our Lord and Savior Jesus Christ. (2 Peter 3:18).

 © Sylvia Gunter 2017, The Father's Business P.O. Box 380333 Birmingham, AL 35238

Adoption

"All the days ordained for me were written in your book before one of them came to be. How precious to me are your thoughts, O God, how vast is the sum of them" (Ps. 139:16-17).

God created you because He wanted you. He has watched over you and nurtured you from the womb (Job 10:12). You have never been alone or unloved. Your life is not a random thing. Adoption was not God's plan B. He chose both your biological parents and your adopted parents. He chose every part of the script of your life.

God thought through all the details—your siblings, your birth order, large family or small family. He foresaw your pain, too. Allow the comforting presence of Jesus to touch and heal any wounded place. Be blessed to bring Him all of your unanswered questions. Rest in His perfect care of you. Be blessed as His love validates and affirms that you are His. His thoughts of you are precious and too vast to count. You are His special covenant child. God has given you everything you need to be an overcomer and to live in the beauty of all that He placed within you.

In God's master plan He chose your spiritual heritage. Your generational blessings go back a thousand generations (Deu. 7:9). As an adopted child you receive a double portion. You have the generational blessings of your biological parents and your adopted parents. He chose this spiritual treasure chest of blessings for you.

God pours out His lovingkindness on you every day in big ways and little ways. You are blessed by your Father who has carried you until you reached this place (Deu. 1:31).

Because of His love, His power, and His blessing, He can cause all the events of your life to be transformed in His story of you. This is your story: You are loved with an everlasting love by a perfect heavenly Father. He is looking forward to revealing the chapters of the story He has already written just for you. He celebrates who you are. Be blessed to hear the song that your Father rejoices to sing over you (Zeph. 3:17).

Daughter

"The king is enthralled by your beauty; honor him, for he is your lord. All glorious is the princess within her chamber; her gown is interwoven with gold" (Ps. 45:11,13).

You are an amazing daughter. God rejoiced as He gave you to our family as a gift. As much as I love you, God loves you more with a love that is deeper, wider, and higher than you can imagine (Eph. 3:18).

Be blessed to see yourself as God sees you. You are a glorious princess, and the King is enthralled with your beauty. He is captivated by you. He likes you just the way you are. May you quickly recognize any negative thoughts or words as a tool of the enemy and replace them with this truth: You are a beloved daughter of your loving heavenly Father (Rom. 8:16).

God has always been with you. His zealous love and care have kept guard over your spirit (Job 10:12). There has never been a day when you were alone. He will never leave you or forsake you. Even when you mess up, Jesus will restore you to complete wholeness through His mercy and grace. Nothing can separate you from His love.

Allow God to mold you to be more like Jesus. Be quick to hear God's voice and follow where He leads. May God's Spirit of truth help you rejoice in what is good and detest what is evil (Ps. 1). God is more than enough to satisfy every longing of your heart.

I rejoice in who you are and in the woman that you are becoming. You are a reflection of God's lovingkindness and tender mercy. His plans for you are more than you can ask or imagine. Pursue God-sized dreams and follow after Him with all your heart.

My greatest desire for you is that you act justly, love mercy, and walk humbly with your God (Micah 6:8). He knows what is best for you, so I release you to Him. May God continue to show His favor all the days of your life.

 © Sylvia Gunter 2017, The Father's Business P.O. Box 380333 Birmingham, AL 35238

Son

"And a voice from heaven said, 'This is my Son, whom I love; with him I am well pleased'" (Matt. 3:17).

You are a wonderful son. God gave you to our family as a gift. He has been with you since He knit you together in the womb. On the day you were born, heaven rejoiced. I love you. As much as I love you, God loves you more. He loves you with love that is deeper, wider, and higher than you can imagine.

You are a beloved son, and God is your loving Father. You are created in the image of Him who is called Warrior (Exo. 15:3). Be blessed to see yourself as God sees you. You have everything you need to succeed because He is with you. Recognize any negative thoughts or words as a tool of the enemy and replace them with this truth: I am a son who pleases God.

His zealous love and care have kept guard over your spirit like a shepherd keeps watch over his sheep (Job 10:12). There is never a day when you are alone. He will never leave you or forsake you. Even when you mess up, Jesus is waiting to restore you completely in Him. Nothing can separate you from His love.

Allow God to mold you to be more like Jesus. Be quick to hear His voice and follow where He leads. May God's Spirit of truth help you rejoice in what is good and detest what is evil (Ps. 1).

I rejoice in who you are and in the man you are becoming. You reflect God's Father-heart. Be blessed as you share your strength with those around you. You have been set apart for God. He is inviting you to join Him on an adventure that is beyond what you can ask or imagine.

My greatest desire for you is that you act justly, love mercy, and walk humbly with your God (Micah 6:8). He knows what is best for you, so I release you to Him. May God continue to show His favor all the days of your life.

Wandering Child

"May you know God. May you progressively become more deeply and intimately acquainted with Him, recognizing and understanding the wonders of His Person more strongly and clearly. May you come to know the power outflowing from His resurrection which it exerts over believers. May you so share His sufferings as to be continually transformed in spirit into His likeness" (2 Peter 3:18, Amplified).

May God open your eyes and awaken your spirit to His great love. May His love take root and grow deeply in your heart that you may know Him.

In areas where you have wandered far from home, be blessed to "come to yourself" as the prodigal son did in a distant land and return to your Father (Luke 15:17). Your heavenly Father is waiting expectantly for you.

Painful experiences may have skewed your view of God. Be blessed with the healing love and compassion of Jesus touching everything from the past. May your spirit and soul see things as they are from God's spiritual insight and understanding (Col. 1:9-14). Allow the Holy Spirit to minister God's truth and bring you into His light.

May the wounded places in you be blessed with God's comfort for all negative emotions. Your tender Abba can heal them all. He feeds you with gentleness and kindness, nourishing you with hope in Him, drawing you deeper into His grace.

Nothing you have done can change His love for you. The righteousness of Christ covers all faults and failure. Jesus gave Himself to make you clean and blameless. Allow His power to release you from anything that has kept you in bondage. Be blessed to receive His complete and unconditional love.

© Sylvia Gunter 2017, The Father's Business P.O. Box 380333 Birmingham, AL 35238

Mom

"Her children rise and call her blessed" (Pro. 31:28).

Mom, God created the family and the roles of mother and father as a reflection of who He is. Thank you, Mom, for the ways you have shown both God's tenderness and strength. Your lovingkindness makes the good times brighter and the trying times easier. You are a blessing that no one can replace.

So much of what you do is not seen by others. Be blessed to know that God sees everything. Receive the hope of His reward for the many hours spent praying, serving, and loving your family (Matt. 6:18b). May God richly bless you for the many thankless tasks and just plain hard work. Hear your Father say, "Well done, good and faithful servant. I love you. I am well pleased with you" (Matt. 25:23; Matt. 3:17).

You may have felt at times that your identity is what you do: diaper-changer, taxi-driver, cook, or caregiver. Be blessed to hear your Father speak to you of your true identity. You are your Beloved's and He is yours (Song 6:3). You are deeply loved and cherished by God simply because of who you are. Be blessed to sense how He celebrates you.

You are a mother to both physical and spiritual children. Many benefit from the gift of who you are. May every godly seed that you have planted in the lives of others bear fruit in multiplied ways. You are making a larger impact than you can comprehend. Be at peace knowing your generational legacy is secure. God shows His love to a thousand generations of those who love Him and keep His commandments. Stay faithful to who God has made you to be, and He will do the rest.

Be blessed to continue to walk in the light of Jesus so that His name and renown may be magnified in the coming generations. Be blessed as you carry the holy blessing of His presence with you every place you go.

Dad

God created the family and the roles of mother and father as a reflection of who He is. Thank you for the ways you have shown God's Father-heart. You have demonstrated God's strength, wisdom, and protection. I am proud to call you Dad.

While you may have felt at times that your identity is what you do, be blessed to hear your Father speak to you of your true identity. You are the beloved, deeply loved and cherished by God simply because of who you are. You are a delight to Him.

No one can fully appreciate the heavy weight you carry of being provider and protector. Allow God to strengthen and sustain you in all the pressures of stewarding your family. Receive His Spirit of wisdom and understanding, so that you take only His yoke upon you. His yoke is easy, and His burden is light. You can be confident in His ability and presence to work in everything that concerns you. You have His favor and blessing as a shield.

So much of what you do is not seen by others. Be blessed to know that God sees everything. Receive the hope of His reward for the many hours spent working, praying, serving, and loving your family (Matt. 6:18). May God richly bless you for many thankless tasks and just plain hard work. Hear your Father say of you, "Well done, good and faithful servant. I love you. You are my son. I am well pleased with you" (Matt. 25:23; Matt. 3:17).

You are a father to both physical and spiritual children. Many benefit from the gift of who you are. May every godly seed that you have planted in the lives of others bear fruit in multiplied ways. You are making a larger impact than you can comprehend. Be at peace knowing your generational legacy is secure. God shows His love to a thousand generations of those who love Him and keep His commandments. Stay faithful to who God has made you to be, and He will do the rest. Be blessed as you carry the blessing of His presence with you every place you go.

 © Sylvia Gunter 2017, The Father's Business P.O. Box 380333 Birmingham, AL 35238

Birthday

"Like an open book, you watched me grow from conception to birth; all the stages of my life were spread out before you, the days of my life all prepared before I've even lived one day" (Ps. 139:16, Message).

God knew everything about you before your birth. He was there the day you were born, and He rejoiced over you with singing (Zeph. 3:17). You are precious to God. He chose you before the foundation of the world to be adopted into His family (Eph. 1:4-5).

Today I celebrate you. You are fearfully and wonderfully made. You bear the imprint of God's fingerprints in your spirit, soul, and body. You are a reflection of His creativity. Everything about you—your personality, the way you see and interact with the world, and your outward appearance—were all handpicked by God. You are a masterpiece.

Your birth and life were appointed before time for good works, which God prepared for you to walk in for His glory. You were not an accident. He created you for a specific purpose. His plans for you are to prosper you and give you hope and a future. Be blessed to feel confident and ready for the year ahead, with God ordering your steps. Be blessed to find joy in every circumstance, knowing that He is working for your good.

God has given you the greatest gift: abundant life in Christ. Be blessed to pursue the fullness of His abundance. His dreams and plans for you are more than you could ask or imagine. All God's promises are yes and amen for you.

Today be blessed to feel how deeply loved you are by God. He likes you. In fact, He adores you. You are His special treasure. Be blessed with deep and abiding joy as a favored child of Most High God. May this day and all your days be filled with the wonder of God's special love for you.

© Sylvia Gunter 2017, The Father's Business P.O. Box 380333 Birmingham, AL 35238

Friend

"It is right and appropriate for me to have this confidence and feel this way about you all, because you have me in your heart and I hold you in my heart as partakers and sharers, one and all with me, of God's grace" (Phil. 1:7a, Amplified).

Precious friend, you are a special person who brings life and joy to many. Your friendship is a treasured gift from God. It is a tangible representation of His love and care. God blessed me when you came into my life. You have made a home in my heart and I in yours. May we be blessed to walk together in Jesus so we can have true fellowship of spirit with each other (1 John 1:7).

You are the display of God's splendor. The way you listen to others and hear what they are truly saying displays God's kindness and attentiveness. Your strong faith allows you to share God's strength with others, showing His protection and care. Your smile and laughter exude the joy of the Lord and echo the pleasure God has in us.

Jesus delights to call you His friend. He has revealed to you everything that He has heard from His Father (John 15:15). Be blessed with ears that hear His sweet voice and a heart that receives what He says. Jesus is your truest friend who sticks closer than a brother (Pro. 18:24). He laid down His life for you, His friend (John 15:13). He is always with you.

I am honored to be one of the cloud of witnesses cheering you on as your run your race. May you fully experience the abundant life Christ has given to you. Be filled with the wonder of God's special love for you. You are His special treasure.

Be blessed as your roots go down deep into God's marvelous love. May you be able to feel and understand how long, how wide, how deep and how high God's love is for you (Eph. 3:14-19). He adores you. In you He is well pleased.

 © Sylvia Gunter 2017, The Father's Business P.O. Box 380333 Birmingham, AL 35238

Fruit Of The Spirit

"the fruit of the Spirit is love, joy, peace, patience, kindness, goodness, faithfulness, gentleness and self-control" (Gal. 5:22-23).

The fruit of the spirit is not an emotional response. It is God in you. Be blessed to keep in step with His Spirit and draw on who He is.

Be blessed with God's love that gives freely without asking anything in return. Be blessed with increasing and overflowing love for others.

Be blessed with the joy of the Lord that gives you strength. Be blessed to brighten and refresh weary hearts with the joy of Jesus.

Be blessed with receiving the Lord of peace who is with you always dispensing His peace to you.

Be blessed with grace-filled patience, not just tolerance. Be blessed with God's patient endurance in battles long fought.

God's kindness leads to repentance. Be blessed to pass on that kindness to others. Be blessed with His grace softening all that could be harsh.

Be blessed with active goodness that does not think to repay evil but considers how to bless from the goodness of Jesus in you.

Be blessed in His faithfulness that bears all things, believes all things, hopes all things, and endures all things

Be blessed with the gentle answer of Jesus that turns away wrath. Be blessed with being wise as a serpent but gentle as a dove.

Ponder the immense self-control of Jesus. When He was taunted and crucified, He uttered only forgiveness. Be blessed with a disposition that is even-tempered and in step with His in spirit.

© Sylvia Gunter 2017, The Father's Business P.O. Box 380333 Birmingham, AL 35238

Appendix

© Sylvia Gunter 2017, The Father's Business P.O. Box 380333 Birmingham, AL 35238

Frequently Asked Questions

Can we bless our own spirit?

These blessings are designed for one person to read to another or for you to read to yourself. It is a matter of personal preference. Some people receive well by reading/speaking the blessing to their own spirit. Some people find it to easier to receive if someone else reads/speaks the blessing to them. Try reading them for yourself or get a partner to bless you and see what works best for you.

Can I bless a non-believer?

Whether you are a believer or not, you have a human spirit. Everyone is hungry for validation and acceptance. Blessing is a great way to show pre-Christians the true source of unconditional love in God. The Holy Spirit is at work drawing people to Jesus. Blessing the spirit of a pre-Christian invites their spirit to be open to the invitation of a personal relationship with Jesus. One of the most common things I bless non-believers with comes from the story of the prodigal son. The story in Luke 15 says when the prodigal son came to himself he returned to his father. I often bless non-believers "to come to yourself and return to your Father." Many non Christians are open if you ask "May I bless you?" If they say no, then don't do it. If they are open, keep your blessing short and use everyday language.

Is there a difference between prayer and blessing?

Blessing the spirit does not replace prayer. Blessing is simply another tool in our toolbox that we can use to minister to ourselves and others. Jesus tells us to do both in Luke 6:28. "Bless those who curse you, pray for those who mistreat you." In his letters, the apostle Paul blessed people and prayed for people.

How do I know it is working?

I have heard more than once "I tried reading a blessing once and it didn't work." Many people do respond the first time they receive a blessing, but that is not always the case. Like with prayer, you don't always pray about something once and see instant results. Obedience is your part, results are God's. Be faithful to bless others as you feel led by God. If you speak the truth of God to someone's spirit, you can rest assured that God promises will not return to Him void. Continue to bless the person knowing that God is up to far more that we can see.

Can I bless someone at a distance or without them knowing it?

We can bless someone who is not present, the same way prayer works without the person being present. As with other types of prayer, there is a difference when the recipient hears the words. Consider the difference between telling someone "I'll pray for you" and doing it later, versus taking the time to pray for them in that moment. The same is true when blessing someone's spirit because the soul and body hears the words as well.

© Sylvia Gunter 2017, The Father's Business P.O. Box 380333 Birmingham, AL 35238

Scriptures About The Human Spirit

Gen. 2:7 And the LORD God formed man of the dust of the ground, and breathed into his nostrils the breath [or spirit] of life.

Exo. 35:21 Then everyone came whose heart was stirred, and everyone whose spirit was willing, and they brought the LORD's offering for the work of the tabernacle of meeting...

Num. 14:24 Because my servant Caleb has a different spirit and follows me wholeheartedly...

1 Sam. 1:15 NKJV Hannah answered, "No, my lord, I am a woman of sorrowful spirit. I have drunk neither wine nor intoxicating drink, but have poured out my soul before the LORD.

Ezra 1:1 NKJV The LORD stirred up the spirit of Cyrus king of Persia, so that he made a proclamation throughout all his kingdom, and also put it in writing…

Job 7:11 "Therefore I will not keep silent; I will speak out in the anguish of my spirit, I will complain in the bitterness of my soul.

Job 10:12 You gave me life and showed me kindness, and in your providence watched over my spirit.

Ps. 34:18 The LORD is close to the brokenhearted and saves those who are crushed in spirit.

Ps. 51:10 Create in me a pure heart, O God, and renew a steadfast spirit within me. 12 Restore to me the joy of your salvation and grant me a willing spirit, to sustain me.

Ps. 77:6 I remembered my songs in the night. My heart mused and my spirit inquired...

Ps. 143:4 Therefore my spirit is overwhelmed within me; My heart within me is distressed.

Pro. 11:13 He who is of a faithful spirit conceals a matter.

Pro. 15:13 A happy heart makes the face cheerful, but heartache crushes the spirit.

Pro. 16:18 Pride goes before destruction, a haughty spirit before a fall.

Prov 16:32 NKJV He who is slow to anger is better than the mighty, and he who rules his spirit than he who takes a city.

Pro. 17:22 A cheerful heart is good medicine, but a crushed spirit dries up the bones.

Pro. 17:27 NKJV He who has knowledge spares his words, and a man of understanding is of a calm spirit.

Pro. 20:27 The lamp of the LORD searches the spirit of a man; it searches out his inmost being.

Pro. 25:28 NKJV Whoever has no rule over his own spirit is like a city broken down, without walls.

Pro. 29:23 The humble in spirit will retain honor.

Eccl. 7:8 NKJV The patient in spirit is better than the proud in spirit.

Isa. 26:9 My soul yearns for you in the night; in the morning my spirit longs for you.

Isa. 54:6 The LORD will call you back as if you were a wife deserted and distressed in spirit—a wife who married young, only to be rejected," says your God.

Isa. 57:15 I live in a high and holy place, but also with him who is contrite and lowly in spirit, to revive the spirit of the lowly and to revive the heart of the contrite.

Isa. 61:3 NKJV To console those who mourn in Zion, to give them beauty for ashes, the oil of joy for mourning, the garment of praise for the spirit of heaviness; That they may be called trees of righteousness, the planting of the LORD, that He may be glorified.

 © Sylvia Gunter 2017, The Father's Business P.O. Box 380333 Birmingham, AL 35238

Isa. 66:2 This is the one I esteem: he who is humble and contrite in spirit, and trembles at my word.

Eze. 36:26 I will give you a new heart and put a new spirit in you; I will remove from you your heart of stone and give you a heart of flesh.

Dan. 6:3 Daniel distinguished himself above the governors and satraps, because an excellent spirit was in him; and the king gave thought to setting him over the whole realm.

Zech. 12:1 Thus says the LORD, who … forms the spirit of man within him.

Mal. 2:15-16 So guard yourself in your spirit, and do not break faith with the wife of your youth…

Mark 2:8 Immediately Jesus knew in his spirit that this was what they were thinking in their hearts, and he said to them, "Why are you thinking these things?"

Mark 8:12 NKJV But He sighed deeply in His spirit…

Mark 14:38 "Watch and pray so that you will not fall into temptation. The spirit is willing, but the body is weak."

Luke 1:46-47 "My soul glorifies the Lord and my spirit rejoices in God my Savior.

Luke 1:80 And the child grew and became strong in spirit. (speaking of John)

Luke 2:40 NKJV And the Child grew and became strong in spirit, filled with wisdom; and the grace of God was upon Him. (speaking of Jesus)

Luke 23:46 Jesus called out with a loud voice, "Father, into your hands I commit my spirit." When he had said this, he breathed his last.

John 4:23-24 "Yet a time is coming and has now come when the true worshipers will worship the Father in spirit and truth, for they are the kind of worshipers the Father seeks. God is spirit, and his worshipers must worship in spirit and in truth."

John 11:33 When Jesus saw her weeping, and the Jews who had come along with her also weeping, he was deeply moved in spirit and troubled.

John 13:21 After he had said this, Jesus was troubled in spirit and testified, "I tell you the truth, one of you is going to betray me."

John 19:30 Jesus bowed his head and gave up his spirit.

Acts 7:59 While they were stoning him, Stephen prayed, "Lord Jesus, receive my spirit."

Acts 17:16 NKJV Now while Paul waited for them at Athens, his spirit was provoked within him when he saw that the city was given over to idols.

Acts 18:25 NKJV This man had been instructed in the way of the Lord; and being fervent in spirit, he spoke and taught accurately the things of the Lord…

Rom. 1:9 NKJV God is my witness, whom I serve with my spirit in the gospel of His Son, that without ceasing I make mention of you always in my prayers…

Rom. 8:16 The Spirit himself testifies with our spirit that we are God's children.

Rom. 12:11 NKJV…not lagging in diligence, fervent in spirit, serving the Lord;

1 Cor. 2:11 (Amplified) For what person perceives (knows and understands) what passes through a man's thoughts except the man's own spirit within him? Just so no one discerns (comes to know and comprehend) the thoughts of God except the Spirit of God.

1 Cor. 6:20 For you were bought at a price; therefore glorify God in your body and in your spirit, which are God's.

© Sylvia Gunter 2017, The Father's Business P.O. Box 380333 Birmingham, AL 35238

1 Cor. 7:34 An unmarried woman or virgin is concerned about the Lord's affairs: Her aim is to be devoted to the Lord in both body and spirit.

1 Cor. 14:15 I will pray with my spirit, but I will also pray with my mind; I will sing with my spirit, but I will also sing with my mind.

2 Cor. 2:13 NKJV I had no rest in my spirit, because I did not find Titus my brother.

2 Cor. 7:1 Since we have these promises, dear friends, let us purify ourselves from everything that contaminates body and spirit, perfecting holiness out of reverence for God.

2 Cor. 7:13 In addition to our own encouragement, we were especially delighted to see how happy Titus was, because his spirit has been refreshed by all of you.

1 Thess. 5:23 (GOD'S WORD) May the God who gives peace make you holy in every way. May he keep your whole being—spirit, soul, and body—blameless when our Lord Jesus comes.

Heb. 4:12 For the word of God is living and active. Sharper than any double-edged sword, it penetrates even to dividing soul and spirit, joints and marrow; it judges the thoughts and attitudes of the heart.

1 Peter 3:4 …let it be the hidden person of the heart, with the incorruptible beauty of a gentle and quiet spirit, which is very precious in the sight of God.

More Books by Sylvia Gunter

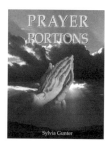

Prayer Portions is a resource manual for all who are seeking God's heart and asking, "Lord, teach me to pray." 8½ x 11 inches, 366 pages, 156 prayer resources, tools, and strategies in sections on praise, repentance, warfare, personal life with God, and intersession. These Scripture-based resources help you develop a lifestyle of praying without ceasing. It is milk for spiritual babes and hearty meat for those who want to grow in prayer. Prayer Portions leads you to see, understand, believe, receive, and enter into God's designs through prayer.

For The Family is 48 pages of powerful prayers for husbands and wives, moms and dads, who want to pray God's heart and see Him glorified in your family. It is full of God's love, grace, and power. It came out of the Refiner's fire of desperation in intercession for families. It is intended for those who need a starting point for intercession for your family and those who need fresh weapons in the battle.

Safe In The Father's Heart: Finding The Father's Love You Have Always Wanted is an invitation to wholeness, peace, and joy as you live in God's delight in you as His child. This book is Sylvia's story of discovering and experiencing the Father heart of God. Her prayer is that God may speak to the hearts of many. God is powerful enough to create the universe and personal enough to delight in holding you in His Father heart. He is waiting to show you the depths of His love for you.

© Sylvia Gunter 2017, The Father's Business P.O. Box 380333 Birmingham, AL 35238

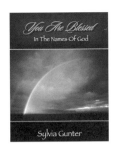

You Are Blessed In The Names Of God is 8½ x 11 inches, 224 pages, with 112 blessings and 32 pages of teaching. My passion is to see people living in the fullness of their God-given design. "May God himself, the God of peace, sanctify you through and through. May your whole spirit, soul, and body be kept blameless at the coming of our Lord Jesus Christ" (1 Thes 5:23). Husbands and wives are blessing each other. Parents are blessing children. Teachers are blessing students. Counselors are blessing clients, and friends are blessing friends. God meets His children at their place of need through blessings.

Revealing The Treasures guides you deeper into your identity in Christ and experience with God. It answers the question of "Who is God and who I am in Christ because of who He is?" Our Creator and Designer is the source of answers to our search for identity, legitimacy, meaning and significance. Your heart will meet Him in transforming truth.

Free To Be You— by Elizabeth Gunter
Your Creator intricately designed the masterpiece of you. He is longing for you to discover the joy of living out of everything He has put in you. *Free To Be You* is a study of the seven gifts from Romans 12. For each gift there is a profile, a Biblical character study, an interview with a person having that gift, and a blessing for the gift. Get beyond what you do to why you do what you do. Be free to be you.

For all the resources available
from Sylvia Gunter and Elizabeth Gunter and to order
go to **www.thefathersbusiness.com**
Email info@thefathersbusiness.com • 205-980-8382

© Sylvia Gunter 2017, The Father's Business P.O. Box 380333 Birmingham, AL 35238

© Sylvia Gunter 2017, The Father's Business P.O. Box 380333 Birmingham, AL 35238